NO. 61

UNIVERSITY OF MINNESOTA PAMPHLETS

ON AMERICAN WRITERS   65 CENTS

Sarah Orne Jewett

BY MARGARET FARRAND THORP

PAMPHLETS ON AMERICAN WRITERS · NUMBER 61

UNIVERSITY OF MINNESOTA

Sarah Orne Jewett

BY MARGARET FARRAND THORP

UNIVERSITY OF MINNESOTA PRESS · MINNEAPOLIS

© Copyright 1966 by the University of Minnesota

Printed in the United States of America at the
Jones Press, Minneapolis

3 2

Library of Congress Catalog Card Number: 66-64594

PUBLISHED IN GREAT BRITAIN, INDIA, AND PAKISTAN BY THE OXFORD
UNIVERSITY PRESS, LONDON, BOMBAY, AND KARACHI, AND IN CANADA
BY THE COPP CLARK PUBLISHING CO. LIMITED, TORONTO

SARAH ORNE JEWETT

MARGARET FARRAND THORP, who is the wife of Professor Willard Thorp of Princeton University, is the author of a number of books, among them *Female Persuasion: Six Strong-Minded Women* and *The Literary Sculptors*. With her husband she edited *Modern Writing*.

⤎ *Sarah Orne Jewett*

Anyone from another part of the United States, anyone from another part of the world, who wants to understand New England might do well to begin with the stories of Sarah Orne Jewett. These subtle "sketches," as she called them, do not contain the whole of New England but they distill its essence. Here are the qualities which made New England great, which spread its influence across the continent, which had so much to do with the shaping of those midwesterners who, Miss Jewett herself thought, would be the typical Americans of the future.

⌈Miss Jewett was an integral part of the society she described.⌉ Her father was a country doctor, her grandfather a sea captain and an owner of merchant ships. The Jewett family was important in the community of South Berwick, Maine. Among her relatives Sarah Jewett could study most of the New England traits she liked to dwell on: a sense of duty (writing she came to think was her duty), independence, courage, endurance, an enjoyment of work, an imperious conscience.

Her sketches set these qualities in many different lights though she does not deliberately begin with a characteristic and build her story on that. She starts with a character or a place and the virtue, sometimes not even named, appears along the way. In "The Hiltons' Holiday," for instance, "the magnitude of the plan for taking a whole day of pleasure confronted [John Hilton] seriously." Again, in "An Autumn Holiday" the narrator (Miss Jewett herself) makes an unexpected call on two elderly sisters and finds them walking back and forth at their spinning wheels.

They insist on stopping so that they may talk more comfortably with their guest but each as she sits down takes up her knitting for "neither of them were ever known to be idle."

The humorous side of these serious virtues Miss Jewett often enjoyed pointing out and she was well aware also that they have their unlovely aspects. She does not dwell on these, or on the hidden passions in New England life, but she knew that they were there. When the title character of her *Country Doctor* tells a medical friend from the city a curious story about his ward's mother, the visitor exclaims, "I tell you, Leslie, that for intense, self-centred, smouldering volcanoes of humanity, New England cannot be matched the world over." Miss Jewett had often seen the volcanoes of which Robinson, Frost, O'Neill, and some of her other successors would write at length, but these were not the phenomena she wished to study.

What she did want to accomplish in her sketches she liked to explain by a dictum of Plato's: that the best thing one can do for the people of a state is to make them acquainted with one another. She wrote her first book because she wanted to do this for her own state of Maine, to explain its natives to the summer visitors from other parts of the country who disturbed her by the way they misunderstood her neighbors. She did not like to hear people laugh at eccentricities which she knew were, more often than not, indications of admirable qualities. She found that she had the power to elucidate her neighbors and to make people like them; and doing this in writing she enjoyed. She understood her world more deeply than most of her contemporaries because her responses to it were more delicate and subtle. One is constantly struck by this as one reads her; what she sets down are not the observations of a reporter but impressions recollected in tranquillity. Her memory is very sure and strong for details of appearance, of voice, of manner. She may not have

6

been able to trace back to its source each trait with which she built up a character but she knew that each trait was true.

With an equal fidelity she remembered vividly all sorts of sense impressions: the color of marsh rosemary — "the grey primness of the plant is made up from a hundred colors"; the quality of a song sparrow's note; the mingled scents of balsam, fir, and bayberry coming over salt water. Her sense of smell was particularly keen. She did not describe a landscape; she created it from remembered pieces so that many of her readers were sure they knew exactly which village or stretch of seacoast she had in mind — and were always wrong. It is this power of re-creating impressions which makes Sarah Jewett something a little larger than a local colorist, which makes one want to read her for other reasons beside the desire to comprehend New England. Her Maine people are not simply authentic Down Easters; they are kin to people of other times and places. The funeral procession in *A Country Doctor* might have been "a company of Druid worshipers." Mrs. Hight in "A Dunnet Shepherdess" has "the features of a warlike Roman emperor . . . Her scepter was a palm-leaf fan." In *The Country of the Pointed Firs*, which contains more of the essence of New England than any of her other books, one comes often on allusions of this kind. Mrs. Todd, the herb-woman, who is the narrator's guide to Dunnet Landing, is spoken of as a "huge sibyl," a *caryatide*, an "Antigone alone on the Theban plain." At the annual reunion of the Bowden family, the guests, as they walk from the dinner table to the church "ought to be carrying green branches and singing" as they went.

There was another idea Miss Jewett wanted her stories to demonstrate: the importance of the commonplace. She wanted to write about ordinary life as though she were writing history. "Écrire la vie ordinaire comme on écrit l'histoire." When she came on this maxim of Flaubert's she greeted it at once as a precise statement of what she was trying to do, copied it out, and pinned it over her writing desk. She took deep pleasure in the commonplaces of her own daily existence but she was discriminating in what she enjoyed and this taught her to distinguish in her writing between the significant and the merely precise detail, another point at which she differs from many of the local colorists.

One reason why Sarah Jewett was able to describe New England characteristics accurately was that she had many of them herself. Consider, for instance, the sense of duty, that trait so often puzzling to the outlander who calls it the New England conscience. There is a particularly effective presentation of this in "A Dunnet Shepherdess." The narrator — who comes from Boston to Dunnet Landing — meets Esther Hight, the shepherdess, and learns something of her history.

Esther has been in love for years with William Blackett, a fisherman who lives on one of the outer islands, but she cannot marry him because she must take care of her paralyzed mother. Mrs. Hight, a very energetic woman, had in middle life a stroke which left her almost helpless, except for her left hand. At about the same time her husband died, leaving her a rocky and heavily mortgaged farm. Esther, her only child, was sure that the best use that could be made of the land was sheep farming and set herself to find ways of making that profitable. Her neighbors in the high country above the Landing had been discouraged because so many of their sheep were killed by dogs and Esther became convinced that what was needed was shepherding. Instead of leaving the sheep to shift for themselves in the stony pastures she determined, hard though it might be, to watch over them by day and even on moonlight nights when the dogs were likely to roam about. She had physical as well as moral stamina and her sheep prospered. There was a good route to the Boston market for the wool and her flock became locally famous so that sheep breeders paid well for her lambs. She worked off the mortgage on the farm and began to put money in the bank. The teller of the story learns these facts when William, the fisherman, takes her on a trout-fishing expedition into the high country, and she guesses at the romance though neither of the lovers mentions it.

While Esther and William spend a happy afternoon together the narrator has a long talk with the old mother who puts the situation to her simply: "It has been stubborn work, day and night, summer and winter, an' now she's beginnin' to get along in years . . . She's tended me 'long o' the sheep, an' she's been a good girl right along, but she ought to have been a teacher." This is the way a Maine woman talks of duty. Later there is a revelatory word from Esther herself, speaking to her visitor. " 'I hope you ain't goin' to feel too tired, mother's so deaf; no, I hope you won't be tired,' she said kindly, speaking as if she well knew what tiredness was."

A portrait of courage, endurance, and self-respect is "Going to Shrewsbury." This is chiefly a monologue by old Mrs. Peet who meets on the train a good friend she has not seen for a long while and details all her present circumstances and the reason for her journey. A hard-dealing nephew persuaded her husband, just before his death, to make over the farm to him in payment for a loan. Mrs. Peet will not stay there and be dependent on the hypocritical young man so she is seeking asylum with some nieces in Shrewsbury, but she has no intention of being a burden on anyone. "I've got more work in me now than folks expects at my age." (She is seventy-six.) "I ain't goin' to sag on to nobody."

Another trait frequently puzzling to the outsider, especially if he comes from the South, is the New England capacity, even preference, for solitude. Misanthropy has nothing to do with this state of mind. Most of the solitaries like to mix with people and like to talk but there are other things they value more, independence, the pleasure of being surrounded by their own possessions, freedom to order their lives and do things in their own way. Miss Jewett presents this effectively in "Aunt Cynthy Dallett."

The old widowed aunt lives on a steep hill, many miles above a seaport village. Her spinster niece lives in the village and so is not isolated like her aunt though much of her daily life is spent without company. Each of them is lonely but neither can quite bear to give up her independent way of life. Finally the niece agrees to come up the hill and spend the winter. "I'm beat by age at last," Aunt Cynthy says, "but I've had my own way for eighty-five years, come the month o' March."

Sarah Jewett herself never lived completely alone but many of her greatest pleasures were solitary. She walked alone; she rode alone; she made boating excursions alone on the Piscataqua River. She has left records of many of these expeditions in her essays and some of the stories have their source in an autobiographical journey. But for all her delight in solitude and admiration for many of those who practiced it Sarah Jewett could sympathize with the opposite state of mind. She watched it with affectionate amusement among the Irish immigrants who were beginning to flock into Maine in large numbers. One of her Irish stories, "Bold Words at the Bridge," tells of two neighbors whose violent disagreements brought them almost to blows and who once became so angry with each other that for weeks they refused to speak. Finally they made up because neither of them could endure spending another day in silence.

Of the unhealthy extremes to which the endurance of solitude can go Miss Jewett was aware too. She tells, for instance, the story of "Poor Joanna," the recluse of Shell-heap Island. Joanna was crossed in love and came to believe that her anger with God over her cruel fate was an unpardonable sin. She was not fit, she felt, to live among men so she rowed herself out to a small deserted island where her father had once built a little shack to use on fishing excursions. There for the rest of her life she lived quite alone receiving only a very occasional visitor.

Worse than this, because of its effect on his family, is the cruelty of the solitary "King of Folly Island." While a young man he quarreled so fiercely with his neighbors on political issues that he swore he would never again set foot on any land but his own. He bought an island far out in the bay and lived there alone with his wife and daughter. For twenty-six years he carried on his necessary business with his enemies, the John's Islanders, only by boat. His wife pined and died of loneliness and his daughter weakened with tuberculosis but he would not take her to the mainland and she would not go without him.

Sarah Jewett's preparation for chronicling these people of Maine and their ways began, one might say, with her birth. That event took place on September 3, 1849, in South Berwick, Maine, a strategic little village for her purposes. It is situated on the Piscataqua River, one of those noble tidal rivers so characteristic of Maine which carry the sea inland for many miles. The Piscataqua forms the lower border between Maine and New Hampshire. Just below Berwick it is joined by the Salmon River and the two flow down, some twenty miles, to Portsmouth and the sea.

Berwick was settled in 1627 by Englishmen attracted by the Indians' great salmon fishery and by the fine water power. Above tidewater there is a long succession of falls. Gradually the village grew into an important ship-building center which flourished until the Civil War. After that the life of the community altered sharply. Manufacturing began to replace shipping. Factories were built by the falls, wool and cotton mills first, then a cannery. Irish and French-Canadians came in to work them and a new society began to grow upon the New England foundations. Sarah Jewett saw the whole transformation at intimate range. The old ways seemed to her the better and she wanted to record them as standards.

The house in which she was born and lived for much of her childhood left a strong influence on her tastes. Her grandfather had purchased about 1820 the Haggens house, one of the finest in Berwick. It was built in 1774, admirably built by ship's carpenters. The rooms were well proportioned with some fine paneling. To carve the banisters and newel posts of the handsome staircase and the fluted columns of the arch in the hall had occupied, so the story ran, three men for one hundred days. Much of the furnishings Captain Jewett brought from England. There were Sheraton and Chippendale chairs and tables, Adam mirrors, Lowestoft china. Sarah Jewett grew up in contact with excellence.

The beneficent Providence which set her childhood in precisely the environment which would be of most use to her later, provided her with relatives who furnished the little girl with experiences peculiarly helpful to the future writer. Particularly important in this respect was Grandfather Jewett, the patriarch of the family, in whose house Sarah was born.

Theodore Furber Jewett ran away to sea when he was a boy and found that seamanship was his true vocation. He learned fast and at twenty-four became an able captain, a daring one, too. During the War of 1812 he tried to run a cargo to the Caribbean, was captured by the English and held prisoner for many months.

When he retired from the sea Captain Jewett turned shipowner and merchant, a very successful merchant who built up a substantial fortune to the comfort of his descendants and the benefit of American fiction. It was her share of Grandfather Jewett's legacy which enabled Sarah Jewett to write at leisure and as she pleased. The Captain was a fine teller of tales of adventure to which Sarah listened avidly. She knew all his ships and where they were bound on each voyage. She was full of excitement when one was coming up the river, and when the ship's master came to dine and make his report to her grandfather she took care to be sitting in a quiet corner of the room. She gleaned in this way not only sea stories of all kinds but an intimate knowledge of sea terms and sea speech which her writer's memory registered unconsciously for future use. A general store which Captain Jewett opened in South Berwick provided the future storyteller with another rich mine of Maine speech. The farmers who brought down great logs for the shipyard liked to gather round the stove. They paid small attention to the little girl who sat listening quietly to their talk.

Her grandmother, the Captain's first wife for whom she was named, Sarah knew only as a legend. The lovely Sarah Orne of Portsmouth married the Captain when she was eighteen, bore him two sons, and died in her twenty-fifth year. The grandmother little Sarah knew was the Captain's third wife, a solemn, formal person who disapproved of her granddaughter's manners. There were uncles and aunts, too, with strongly individual New England characters.

Sarah's maternal grandfather was also an influence, though he lived in Exeter, New Hampshire. Dr. William Perry had a high medical reputation and not a little fame as the inventor of a process for making starch from potatoes. Both he and his lively wife sent Sarah constant instruction on what books to read and made her report to them in letters her impressions and criticism.

Sarah's mother, daughter of the Exeter doctor, had, it would seem, that good New England gift called "faculty," which means that everything she turned her hand to she did well: her cakes were always light, her biscuits delicately browned, her rooms well swept and garnished with flowers from her own garden. She seems, too, to have had "faculty" as a mother: her three daughters enjoyed her company and confided in her all through her life.

She was well educated and well read. She taught her girls to enjoy reading aloud and gave them literary as well as domestic standards.

With her two sisters Sarah Jewett's relations were warm and close. Mary was her elder by two years; Caroline six years younger. Of Mary, Laura E. Richards has left, in her *Stepping Westward*, a pleasant portrait. Mary never married but was an indispensable power in her family and in the community. She was not only an excellent housekeeper but an admirable manager of all the business affairs of the family and, in addition to that, knew so much about South Berwick and had such sound judgment in civic matters that the selectmen consulted her on all sorts of problems from the naming of a street to the purchase of fire-fighting apparatus. Sarah Jewett's *A White Heron*, published in 1886, is dedicated to "My dear sister Mary." To her younger sister, Caroline, Sarah Jewett dedicated in 1893 *A Native of Winby*. "I have had many pleasures," the inscription runs, "that were doubled because you shared them and so I write your name at the beginning of this book."

Another strong influence came into Sarah Jewett's life when she was twenty. At Wells she met Theophilus Parsons, emeritus professor of law at Harvard, who became at once a sustaining friend. As an ardent Swedenborgian he helped her own faith and for many years she poured out to him in letters her troubles and problems as well as her joys. He developed a deep affection for her and helped her in every way he could.

But the person whom Sarah Jewett loved best and whose influence on her was strongest was her father, the Captain's second son, Dr. Theodore Herman Jewett. Theodore Jewett graduated from Bowdoin, studied medicine in Exeter under Dr. Perry and at Jefferson Medical College in Philadelphia where he took his degree. When he had married Dr. Perry's daughter and was ready to establish a practice of his own, he would have preferred to live in some large city where he might keep in touch with the new developments in medicine which interested him greatly but, to please his father, he settled in Berwick and became a country doctor. He never regretted the decision. He enjoyed all phases of of his work and performed them with extraordinary diligence and skill. He was tireless in his devotion to his patients, answering calls at any hour and in any weather and serving not only as physician but as psychiatrist, family counselor, and confidential friend. His intellectual interest in his profession never slackened; he taught obstetrics at Bowdoin, was president of the Maine Medical Association, wrote frequently for the medical journals, and often made journeys to Boston to talk with colleagues and inform himself on the newest practices in his art. His daughter's portrait of him in *A Country Doctor* may be accepted as accurate, quite without exaggeration.

Sarah's close friendship with her father was a happy product of her serious physical weakness, the arthritis which troubled her all through life. It was diagnosed then as rheumatism and one of the best remedies for it seemed to be fresh air. At any rate since the little girl began to droop whenever she was long indoors, Dr. Jewett encouraged her again and again to take a day off from school and drive about with him on his country visits. Nothing could have been better for her education than her observation of her father's proceedings and her long talks with that wise and compassionate man.

Not unnaturally Sarah came to think that she would like to be a doctor. She was convinced very early that she would never marry. She had all through her life many excellent male friends of all ages but there is no record of even the faintest shadow of a love affair. This state of mind was easily explained by the pre-Freudian nineteenth century. Miss Jewett's County Doctor says of his ward while she is still quite young: "I see plainly that Nan is not the sort of girl who will be likely to marry. When a man or woman has that sort of self-dependence and unnatural self-reliance, it shows itself very early. I believe that it is a mistake for such a woman to marry. . . . and if I make sure by and by, the law of her nature is that she must live alone and work alone, I shall help her to keep it instead of break it, by providing something else than the business of housekeeping and what is called a woman's natural work, for her activity and capacity to spend itself upon."

It seems quite safe to take this as an autobiographical statement. Sarah Jewett thought at first that she could best fulfill the law of her nature by following her father's profession. The obloquy sure to fall on any female who attempted to practice medicine she was quite ready to accept but it soon became apparent to her that she did not have the physical stamina a doctor requires. She had such frequent bouts of illness that she could not be sure of meeting her patients' needs at any hour of the day or night as her father did. Her New England conscience instructed her that she must make herself of real use in the world, but it took her some time to realize that writing was what she was "meant" to do. For many years she thought of it merely as a pleasant avocation.

When she was still a small girl she began to put down on paper the things she was thinking about and the stories she continually told herself when she was alone. She wrote at first in verse because prose frightened her but gradually she found the cadences of prose "more and more enticing" and took that as her true medium.

It was her father, one might say, who really taught her to write, for it was he who taught her to see. As they drove together on his country visits he constantly called her attention to trees, to birds, to flowers, making her look at them until she was familiar with all their details and could thereafter identify them quickly. He made her study houses and people in the same way, and he convinced her that nothing in this world is uninteresting if you only look at it long enough. Little Sarah caught his enthusiasm and looked with interest all her life.

Sarah Jewett's first appearance in print was made in 1868 when she was eighteen. For *The Flag of Our Union*, published in Boston, she wrote a story called "Jenny Garrow's Lovers." This is a fervid melodrama, a form she never tried again. She composed next a simpler, more realistic tale which she sent boldly to the *Atlantic Monthly*. It was rejected but with so encouraging a letter from the editors that she tried again, and was again rejected. Her third attempt was successful. "Mr. Bruce," published in December 1869, is an amusing little story about a very pretty young girl who helps her mother out of an awkward social situation by masquerading as the second-maid and serving the dinner. Romantic complications ensue.

Encouraged by this success Sarah Jewett began to send a stream of stories and poems for children to the juvenile magazines, which printed them and asked for more. She contributed to *Our Young Folks, Merry's Museum, Riverside Magazine for Young People, St. Nicholas, The Independent*, which liked to present some reading for children, and, later, *The Youth's Companion*. In 1873 the *Atlantic* published the first of her Maine stories, "The Shore House," and Sarah Jewett began to feel that writing was her "duty." She kept at it steadily.

Her first book was published in 1877 when she was twenty-eight. It was William Dean Howells who suggested to Miss Jewett that she collect the Maine stories the *Atlantic* had published, rearrange and add to them, and issue them as a book. They were all set in Deephaven, a seaport town which, she was careful to explain in her Preface, she had invented. Both Roberts Brothers and James R. Osgood and Company were ready to publish *Deephaven*. She decided finally on the Osgood firm, which was soon absorbed by the firm now known as Houghton Mifflin. They published most of her other books.

Deephaven does not have a plot in the usual sense of the term. It is a series of impressions of a little Maine coastal town and its inhabitants, as they are received by two lively girls in their early twenties who decide to spend the summer there because one of them has at her disposal the house of a great aunt who has recently died. Miss Brandon was so much respected in Deephaven that everyone welcomes her niece as an old friend. It seems to the young people that the society and way of life of the town are just what they were fifty years ago when it ceased to be an important seaport, but they find this a good way of life, full of interest and devoted to high standards.

The niece's friend, who tells the story, describes first "The Brandon House" (which resembles in many ways the Jewett house in Berwick), its furnishings, its treasures, its memories. Then she gives accounts of the various kinds of people she and her friend come to know in the town: "My Lady Brandon and the Widow Jim," "Deephaven Society," "The Captains." The sketches present individuals of different types and the girls' relations with them. We listen to their conversation and hear the stories they tell, ranging from the history of their neighbors to adventures at sea to tales of second sight. There are Miss Brandon's aristocratic friends; there are old sailors — each must be addressed as Captain; there are fishermen; there are housewives of various degrees of social importance. The men are full of wisdom and salty talk, but they tend to blur a little into one another. The women are more distinctive. There is the lady of the old school, Miss Honora. There is the Widow Jim who has "an uncommon facility of speech" but has endured, courageously, hard years with a drunken husband and is known as "a willin' woman," always respected. There is Mrs. Bonny who comes down from the hills in the summertime riding on her rough-coated old horse with bags and baskets of "rosbries" tied to the saddle. There is old Miss Chauncey, her mind so dim that she thinks herself still rich and elegant as she lives in her denuded, neglected old house, sustained by the charity of her neighbors. There is Mrs. Kew, the lighthouse keeper's wife, with a fine original gift of wit and speech.

There are lively accounts, too, of "Cunner-Fishing," of sailing and cross-country walking, of going to church, attending a lecture, driving to "The Circus at Denby" where the girls hear an illuminating conversation between the Kentucky Giantess and the lighthouse keeper's wife, who had gone to school together.

There seems to be no particular order in the telling of events or in the presentation of characters — that was an art Miss Jewett learned much later — but the young women's enthusiasm for their new friends and new experiences is refreshing and contagious. The tempo and tone of the town become very clear.

The device by which she held these people and events together Miss Jewett was to use again and again. It bears some resemblance, though it is less subtle, to Henry James's central intelligence. A visitor — usually a woman — from Boston or some other part of the outside world comes to Maine and settles for a time in Deephaven, or Grafton, or Dunnet Landing. She meets the most interesting inhabitants of the village, learns their histories, and often makes them into friends. She delights in the old houses she visits and is captivated by the beauty of the austere fields, woods, and sea, so that she presents both narrative and background.

In *Deephaven*, unfortunately, the actual narrator, who is fairly self-effacing, is concerned not only to tell her stories but to make us love her companion, Kate, and admire the way in which she endears herself to different types of people. This puts, from time to time, more emphasis on the double central intelligence than is good for it, but the device of an observer slightly detached but interested is admirable. The weakness is that this central intelligence cannot really function alone; too many of the episodes to be related occurred long before her arrival. It becomes necessary to add an assistant intelligence, an older relative or some long-time resident of the community who knows all the history and legend and can impart them to an eager newcomer.

As a variant on the summer visitor Miss Jewett liked to send back to Maine someone who had roots there but had not lived in the state for a long time. Important among these is the "Native of Winby," now senator from Kansota, who makes a surprise visit to his old school and then to an elderly widow whom he might once have married.

Nineteen years later, when she was writing *The Country of the Pointed Firs* (1896), Miss Jewett was using her visitor device with real skill. The intelligence there is a woman from Boston who has settled in Dunnet Landing as a quiet place to write during the summer. Her response to the people and the stories she encounters is swift and warm but this is not insisted on, as it is in *Deephaven*; it is only implied, so that she does not intrude upon the tale she is telling. Involvement and detachment are beautifully balanced. The assistant narrator, the local herbwoman, is the most interesting of all the narrator assistants, one of the best characters, in fact, Miss Jewett ever drew.

Another literary instrument for which she was to be much admired Miss Jewett used first in *Deephaven*: her accurate and effective employment of Maine speech. Her ear and her memory had been recording it unconsciously ever since she was a little girl and when she came to reproduce it on the printed page she devised a simple method of presenting it to the reader without the cumbersome misspellings so frequently resorted to by the local colorists, even sometimes by a writer as accomplished as Harriet Beecher Stowe.

Miss Jewett's chief tool is the apostrophe, to indicate a dropped final *g* (goin'), or a blurred *a* (same's I always do), or the pronunciation of a word like v'y'ge. She uses it, too, to indicate the shortened vowel sound so characteristic of Maine: co't, bo't, flo't. In addition to this she has a rich knowledge of characteristic words and phrases, some of them very old: "They beseeched me after supper till I let 'em go"; "bespoke"; "master hard"; "master pretty"; "a power of china"; "I'd rather tough it out alone"; "There she goes now, do let's pray her by"; "It allays creeps me cold all over"; "You're gettin' to be as lean as a meetin'-house fly."

One is impressed often by the subtle variations her dialect presents, differences in education and culture, between the young and the very old, between men and women. Sometimes Miss Jewett remarks on the relative social position of two characters she is presenting and this distinction within democracy is reflected by differences in speech.

In the handful of Irish stories the language is not nearly so convincing. Miss Jewett had heard the brogue all her life, chiefly from family servants, but she did not think in it or even, apparently, take an interest in it. As she sets it down it seems correct enough but contrived, not overheard. She records it with a fair amount of restraint but it seems always a little thicker than it ought to be, as though the personages were moving on a stage, not along a country road.

With the occasional French-Canadian characters at whom she tried her hand she is very timid. The Canadians were beginning to come across the border into Maine but not yet to settle, simply to make some money and go home, so that they were not a real part of state life. Of French-Canadian villages Miss Jewett knew something, for she made several trips to Quebec and observed with all her good curiosity the St. Laurent countryside and community life so different from the American. But she did not know it, of course, and what she writes is tentative and generalized. In "Little French Mary," a very slight sketch of a six-year-old daughter of French-Canadians whose pretty affectionate ways charm the old men who sit about the post-office stove in a Maine village, the child has French manners and features but she speaks scarcely two sentences. In "Mère Pochette," set in a French-Canadian village, there is very little dialogue though a good deal of direct report of the dominant character's thinking. The phraseology falls too often into the tiresome form of English translation of the French idiom: "She will be incapable . . . to bring up an infant of no gifts." The story is an uninteresting one, anyway, of a grandmother who finally repents her mistake in breaking up a true love affair.

These dialects never became a serious problem, for Miss Jewett wrote only a few stories about the Irish and the Canadians. What mattered in *Deephaven* and in the later stories was the Maine speech, and her use of that, as I have said, delighted both her readers and the editors who were interested in her literary development. The three particularly concerned to help her were Horace Scudder, at that time editor of the *Riverside*, Howells, the novelist-editor, and Thomas Bailey Aldrich, poet, story writer, and editor of the *Atlantic*, who gave her all the guidance and assistance they could. She asked them many questions and listened with respect to their advice though she did not always follow it. She was quite accurately aware of her own abilities and limitations. One of the points on which she differed with her advisers most strongly was the matter of plot. They urged her to enlarge her sketches to something more nearly resembling the currently popular magazine story and she knew that at that kind of invention she had no skill at all. "I have no dramatic talent," she wrote to Scudder in 1873. "It seems to me I can furnish the theater, and show you the actors and the scenery, but there never is any play." When she tried to make a "play" the result was either sentimental or melodramatic. She contrived sudden inheritances, unfaithful lovers, missing young men who return suddenly rich, wayward daughters who come home to die. There are even thieves and drunkards.

Yet sometimes a preposterous situation produces a convincing story. In "A Lost Lover" all the town of Longfield knows that Miss Horatia had a lover who was lost at sea. The young cousin who comes to visit her one summer is full of curiosity about the romance but Miss Horatia is thoroughly reserved and only a few facts are to be gleaned from Melissa, the devoted family servant. The affair, if it was a real love affair, took place very rapidly many years before when Miss Horatia was on a visit to Salem. The young man went off to sea and his ship was never heard from again.

One morning during the young cousin's visit a tramp comes by asking for food. While he eats he talks freely with Miss Horatia about himself, his bad luck, shipwrecks, craving for drink, and general discouragement. He does not recognize her but she gradually becomes aware who he is. When he leaves she faints, but tells her cousin it is the heat. "God forgive him," she says to herself and takes up her lonely life again.

"The Lost Lover" is an exception. The components of a Jewett story are usually much simpler. The incidents evolve perhaps from two characters in conversation or from a character in relation to an old house or a community. A typical plot is "Miss Tempy's Watchers" in which two elderly women keep the traditional guard, the night before the funeral, over the body of a mutual friend. They install themselves in the kitchen, work at their knitting, and talk about Miss Tempy to whom both of them had been devoted. The circumstances make them speak more openly than they normally would. Nothing happens, but from the conversation emerge three definite and interesting New England characters and some illuminating information on the qualities of generosity and "closeness."

This construction from everyday materials makes the Jewett stories seem more durable than the in many ways comparable tales of Mary E. Wilkins Freeman and Rose Terry Cooke. The plots these writers contrive are ingeniously interesting or amusing, but the joints of their manufacture are too often evident. They are made; they do not grow. Miss Jewett's plots seem inevitable, not something she has invented but something she has seen or overheard or been told of by a friend. It is because she had to manufacture the plots of her Irish and French-Canadian stories that they lack the authenticity of her tales of Maine.

The way in which her Maine stories seemed to grow of themselves never ceased to astonish her. "What a wonderful kind of chemistry it is," she wrote to her close friend Mrs. James T. Fields, "that evolves all the details of a story and writes them presently in one flash of time! For two weeks I have been noticing a certain string of things and having hints of character, etc., and day before yesterday the plan of the story comes into my mind, and in half an hour I have put all the little words and ways into their places and can read it off to myself like print. Who does it? for I grow more and more sure that I don't!"

Her plan of work was to devote her mornings to her large correspondence. She believed firmly that friendships, literary and personal, must be nourished by letters and friendships were an important element in her life. The afternoons were given to the stories. She wrote swiftly and easily, turning out usually two thousand words in an afternoon, sometimes as many as six or seven thousand. A story took form rapidly but after it had got itself down on paper there was still much work to be done. Almost always the first draft was too long; there was an unnecessary amount of detail. She was, as she wrote Scudder, "disposed to longwindedness," but as the years went by she became adept at cutting. It was her French ancestry, she told Mrs. Fields, which made her "nibble all round her stories like a mouse. They used to be as long as yardsticks, they are now as long as spools, and they will soon be the size of old-fashioned peppermints, and have neither beginning or end, but shape and flavor may still be left them." After the cutting Miss Jewett tried to tone down exuberances and push sentimentalities out of sight and, like her admired Flaubert, she labored to find the precise word for every effect she wanted to produce.

The success of *Deephaven* attracted the attention of editors so that soon Miss Jewett was contributing not only to the *Atlantic* but to a number of other magazines, notably *Harper's* and the *Independent*. Her publisher, too, was encouraged to make a collection of her children's stories, *Play Days* (1878), and then began to bring out every few years a volume of selections from her most recent magazine stories. The first of these, *Old Friends and New* (1879), includes "The Lost Lover." Then came *Country By-Ways* (1881) which contains, in addition to stories, several long informal essays. In this genre, which so delighted the nineteenth century and is almost unknown today, Miss Jewett enjoyed working. It gave her opportunity for descriptions of nature, for comment on society and manners, for bits of history and legend, for sketches of good Maine characters. The connecting thread might be as slight as she wished, a horseback ride, a walk, a row on the Piscataqua River, but whatever she treats she treats with skill.

What the modern reader enjoys is the vivid picture she gives him —of a countryside and a community quite different, probably, from anything he has ever lived in but unquestionably authentically described. The disadvantage of the form, so far as Sarah Jewett is concerned, was the temptation it offered to indulge two of her weaknesses: sentimentality and overuse of the pathetic fallacy.

No female writer of the nineteenth century could wholly escape the impulse to sentimentalize but Sarah Jewett, as she grew more mature and more skillful, learned to subdue her sentimentalism effectively. Her overindulgence in the pathetic fallacy was a more personal matter. "The oaks and maples dress themselves as they please, as if they were tired of wearing plain green, like everybody else." The cardinal flowers "keep royal state in the shade, and one imagines that the other flowers and all the weeds at the water's edge take care to bow to them as often as the wind comes by." She wrote that way because trees and flowers and bushes were to her not types and specimens but individual friends. She looked at them as she looked at people. She speaks, for instance, of a row of poplars which she always thought of as cousins.

Country By-Ways is dedicated to "My dear father; my dear friend; the best and wisest man I ever knew." Dr. Jewett had died in 1878 at the age of sixty-three. His heart had been troubling him for a long time but the fatal attack came suddenly and unexpectedly. This was the greatest sorrow Sarah Jewett was ever to know. It was a loss she never ceased to mourn but she was destined, fortunately for her work, to enjoy all through her life the serenity which comes from constant intercourse with a perfectly sympathetic companion. Only a few years after her father's death her horizons were widened and her knowledge increased by her deepening friendship with Mrs. Fields.

Annie Adams at nineteen had married James Fields, seventeen

years her senior and already a prominent member of the firm which would later bear his name, Ticknor and Fields. The marriage was a happy one for American letters; Annie Fields had not only beauty and charm but distinguished gifts as a hostess. Number 148 Charles Street, the Fields Boston home, began at once to flourish as a kind of informal salon, supplemented by the cottage at Manchester-by-the-Sea where they spent their summers. Longfellow, Emerson, Hawthorne, Lowell, Holmes were close friends but the Fields circle was by no means exclusively literary. It included painters, actors, musicians, and men in public life. Many of those who enjoyed the Fields hospitality have set down their impressions of the rich combination of material comforts with good talk.

Fields, who started as an office boy in a Boston bookstore, had risen swiftly to power in the book publishing world. In addition to that, from 1861 to 1870, he edited the *Atlantic Monthly* so that he knew, and knew well, most of the established and the rising literary figures of the day in the United States, in England, and in France. The life in the Charles Street house was a full and happy one until Fields's death in 1881.

Not long after she was left alone Mrs. Fields invited Sarah Jewett to make her an extended visit. Miss Jewett was her junior by fifteen years but they had many tastes and sympathies in common and had already laid the basis for an excellent relationship. Now each found in the other the consolation and companionship she needed and their friendship became rich and sustaining.

Before long it was established that Miss Jewett would spend about three months with Mrs. Fields each winter in the Charles Street house and three in the summer cottage at Manchester, going back to Berwick in between. This kept her in touch with her family and with her country and gave her longer stretches for writing than could be managed in the busy life of Boston. She and Mrs. Fields were assiduous attendants at lectures, plays, and concerts, and Mrs. Fields was a pioneer in Boston charitable work in which Miss Jewett often shared. They liked so much to exchange impressions on everything they read or did that when they were separated they wrote each other little journal notes almost daily. Many of these, included in Mrs. Fields's edition of Miss Jewett's letters, are interesting and illuminating.

The literary hospitality of Charles Street and Manchester continued as in James Fields's lifetime. There were the regular Saturday Afternoons in Boston to which a dozen or so old friends always came as well as new or visiting luminaries. There were small informal lunches and dinners with such friends and neighbors as Dr. Oliver Wendell Holmes, the Lowells, the Aldriches. There were many guests in the seaside cottage.

Mrs. Fields's friends found Miss Jewett a happy addition to the Charles Street circle. She had grown into a distinguished looking young woman, tall and well proportioned with features many people described as beautiful. Elegance is another word which was often applied to her and Mrs. Fields spoke of her "sweet dignity." Sometimes on first sight people thought her formidable but, as she once said, "I seem impressive but actually I only come up to my own shoulder." One was conscious of a point of reserve but she was always straightforward and friendly. She read widely, and her opinions about what she read were fresh and interesting.

The division of time between Boston and Berwick was an excellent arrangement for a writer. Sarah Jewett was able to nibble at and perfect her work to her heart's content because she worked under almost ideal conditions. Few women writers in the nineteenth century found themselves in a comparable situation. She did not need to write for money so the only pressures to hurry or to do too much came from admiring editors who wanted more of her stories. She had no domestic responsibilities. In Boston and Manchester Mrs. Fields had plenty of servants and was accustomed, of course, to direct the household. In Berwick sister Mary did the housekeeping. Sarah was an enthusiastic gardener, she assumed certain household tasks, and she shared for years in the care of her invalid mother, but none of this was very difficult or confining. She could spend, if she liked, the better part of the day at her desk. In neither Boston nor Berwick were there children to disrupt the household. One thinks of Mrs. Stowe, as her son describes her, sitting at the kitchen table trying to dictate to a friend a romantic dialogue for her next installment while she alternately tells a new cook how to season the baked beans and tries to still the clamor of her youngest offspring.

That Mrs. Fields was also engaged in literary work, journals, biographical sketches, the editing of letters, was an incentive to mutual labor and criticism. Sarah Jewett could write as she wanted to, when she wanted to, and between the bouts of work there was stimulating companionship, good talk, reading aloud, and travel.

In 1882 she made her first trip to Europe, with Mrs. Fields. There was another two years later and two more after that. Their routes were for the most part the conventional ones in England, France, and Italy but they were both enthusiastic travelers and made other excursions, into Ireland, Norway, and even Turkey and Greece. What they enjoyed most were the visits to literary friends, old and new. Most exciting of all these were two to Tennyson whom Sarah Jewett thought the greatest man she ever had the privilege of meeting. They took great pleasure also in the Arnolds and the Du Mauriers, in a day with Kipling at Rottingdean and one with Henry James at Rye. Kipling thought Miss Jewett's pictures of New England landscape and New England people corresponded precisely with his own impressions gained in Vermont. James delighted Mrs. Fields by his warm admiration for Miss Jewett's writing.

In the Western hemisphere the two friends did some pioneering in places which have since become standard ground for tourists. They found St. Augustine a delightful town in which to spend part of the winter and in 1896 they joined the Aldriches for a cruise on a friend's yacht in the Caribbean.

The influence of her travel on Miss Jewett's thinking was strong. "You must know the world before you can know the village," she said once to Willa Cather and one is conscious again and again of the light this wider knowledge shed on her view of Maine, but she never attempted a travel book and only occasionally a story without a New England background. There is one not very interesting tale set in St. Augustine, where the local details are carefully accurate, and there are a few unconvincing attempts at pictures of Virginia after the Civil War, too imaginary to be effective. Miss Jewett wrote letters, of course, to friends while she was traveling but, except for some references to people, they are not particularly interesting. Her first impressions of a scene were never so good as those which came after she had thought about it at length.

With her routine thus established Miss Jewett worked happily and well and volumes of collected stories appeared steadily. Eventually there were twelve of them. After the fourth, *The Mate of the Daylight* (1884), she attempted her first novel. She did not suppose that she had developed any skill in plotting but she wanted to make a portrait of her father and the sketch did not give her scope enough. The portrait is interesting and fairly successful; the story is not.

The family setting invented for Dr. Leslie in *A Country Doctor* (1884) is quite different from Dr. Jewett's — Dr. Leslie is a lonely widower, cared for by a faithful servant — but otherwise Sarah

Jewett makes him as like her father as she can. We see him comparing experiences with a much-traveled professional friend, with a charming aged lady he has known from childhood, with patients who desperately need his sympathy and his encouragement as well as his skill, and with others who simply enjoy the importance of being sick. His compassion, adaptability, and quick wit in handling a situation are attractive. His young ward has much the same relation to him that Sarah had to her father but Nan is not an attempt at a self-portrait though she expresses many of Miss Jewett's ideas.

The novel is not well proportioned. The first half, which pictures Nan's early life in the village of Oldfields, is much longer than it needs to be, though it is the best part of the book with its skillful Jewett sketches of country friends and neighbors. There is some of the charm of the later *Country of the Pointed Firs*. The real plot, the choice the heroine makes between marriage and a medical career, at a time when few people thought it possible to combine the two, has the substance for a good novel of the day but the conflict is never made sharp enough to be exciting. Nan realizes very early that she is not the sort of woman intended for matrimony (Sarah Jewett states her own case here, as we have seen) and the young man who would like to dissuade her is too pale a character to seem much of a loss. Other difficulties are not strong enough to be very interesting.

The possibilities she neglected here indicate quite clearly that, though she had vigorous and sometimes radical opinions, Sarah Jewett was not a reformer or a propagandist. She did not want her writing to plead a cause but to explore the relationship between an individual and the life in which he found himself. She did believe, in advance of her time, that a woman had as much right as a man to follow a true vocation but she did not expound this theory often. Her own situation was simple enough, for fiction writing, kept within reasonable limits, was a perfectly proper female occupation.

It was its theme as well as its picture of New England life which made *A Country Doctor* the first of Miss Jewett's books to attract attention abroad. The *Revue des Deux Mondes* (February 1, 1885) published a long review-article by Mme. Thérèse Blanc-Bentzon (she signed herself Th. Bentzon). She thought the book gave, as it does, an excellent picture of New England family life and one of her special concerns was the interpretation of American life to the French. Later, in 1893, she published, with a long Preface, a translation of the novel and of nine of Miss Jewett's stories. The correspondence which grew up between them led to a genuine friendship and each eventually had the pleasure of visiting the other in her home.

Immediately after *A Country Doctor* Miss Jewett tried another novel, *A Marsh Island* (1885). Its proportion and structure are much better than the first novel's, it moves along quite smoothly, but neither the story nor the characters are very interesting. The plot is trite. A well-to-do dilettante landscape painter boards for part of the summer at the marsh island farm. He almost falls in love with the farmer's daughter and enjoys imagining how she would blossom in a richer cultural environment. He almost alienates her from her real lover, a fine metalworker-farmer, whose jealousy is aroused by Doris' interest in the painter. The situation is saved when Doris hears at the last moment that Dan, in his unhappiness, has signed on for a long voyage. She makes a dangerous trip across the marshes in the early morning before the ship leaves to assure him of her true feelings. He does not sail and marries her soon.

The best thing about the novel is its picture of the marsh island farm, isolated and quite different from the others in the neighborhood. The farmer and his wife are estimable hard-working people whom the young painter grows to like and admire but they have little of the savor Miss Jewett usually manages to get into her secondary characters. The contrast between the marsh people and the painter's rich relatives, who are spending the summer further along the coast, has comparatively little force.

Sarah Jewett's only other attempt at a novel was made sixteen years later under the urging of Charles Dudley Warner, the essayist-novelist, who was at that time editing the Hartford *Courant*. He was eager to have her try a story of Berwick in the days of the Revolution and the idea fascinated her because she always wanted to know more about her community's past. As a little girl she had liked to visit the elderly Miss Cushing whose mother had entertained Lafayette and she knew that John Paul Jones had enlisted many Berwick men in the crew of the *Revenge*. *The Tory Lover* (1901), she said, was the hardest year's work she ever did and the year's work she enjoyed most.

The *Atlantic* ran the novel in serial form before its publication as a book and many people liked it despite its faults. The rather violent action — fighting, imprisonments, escapes — was quite beyond Miss Jewett's scope nor was she successful in her attempt to present the complex character of Jones, but the book has two virtues which have not been sufficiently noticed: the talk of the sailors, which Miss Jewett made, probably quite correctly, like the talk of the seafaring men she knew; and the hero, the most lively and attractive young man she ever drew. She sympathized with the conservatism which attached him to the mother country — he enlists with Jones finally to please his lady love — and the exposition of his Tory inclinations is unusual and interesting. The novel was translated not only into French but into Italian and Spanish.

The novels and the hundred or so sketches — her own term is perhaps the best for them — are the most important part of Sarah

Jewett's thirty years of literary labor, particularly the sketches, about seventy of which were reprinted in the collections issued during her lifetime. Interspersed among these were many stories and poems for children and two agreeable books for girls, *Betty Leicester* (1890) and *Betty Leicester's Christmas* (1899). The stories for the very young would probably still amuse the very young of today but Betty Leicester is too unsophisticated for the modern schoolgirl and the moral sentiments in the book are too pointed.

Miss Jewett undertook also, for a series Putnam was publishing for young people, *The Story of the Normans* (1887). She enjoyed the reading she had to do and was apparently unaware how little experience she had in the organization of historical material. There are interesting bits and pieces but it is not a successful book.

Both the juvenile and the adult magazines were happy to print Miss Jewett's verse. She never thought of herself as a poet but sometimes she liked to express ideas in verse rather than through a fictional personality. Most of the adult poems are concerned with the relation of the individual to nature or with some phase of death. In "Top of the Hill," for instance, she is rejoicing in an autumn landscape, observing with pleasure the kind of detail most people would overlook:

> The hedge-rows wear a veil
>   Of glistening spider threads,
> And in the trees along the brook
> The clematis, like whiffs of smoke,
> Its faded garland spreads.

The rhymes for children were numerous but not more than a score of adult poems appeared in print during her lifetime. There were others which she sent in letters to her friends. Mrs. Fields, for instance, received one day a sonnet about a busy, noisy section of Boston where

> I met great Emerson, serene, remote,
> Like one adventuring on seas of thought.

Some years after Miss Jewett's death M. A. De Wolfe Howe arranged a collection of her *Verses* (1916) which were "printed for her friends" by the Merrymount Press in Boston. There are nineteen poems in all here, a few intended for the young, most of the others collected from the *Atlantic, Harper's,* and other journals which had originally printed them. There are also a few which had never been published, notably two on the death of her father who had taught her to look at the world:

> And I must watch the spring this year, alone.

But it was at the perfection of her prose that Sarah Jewett really labored. Some of the devices by which she taught herself to write more effectively we can deduce from her letters to young aspirants who asked her for guidance. If they seemed serious in their work she was generously helpful. "I think," ran one dictum, "we must know what good work is, before we can do good work of our own," and she suggested reading half a dozen really good stories over and over to see *why* they are good. This she did frequently herself, studying with admiration Tolstoi and Turgenev as well as the more usual French and British models. She advised also that if an idea comes into a writer's mind he should try it, see what he can do with it and if it has any value. But chiefly she insisted that "the only way is to keep at work," and this she herself consistently did.

In the successive collections of her stories it is interesting to see how often she improves a later handling of a certain type of subject. One thing she learned, for instance, was that the more she omitted comments of her own and let the humor or poignance of a situation be presented by one of the actors in the story, the more surely she achieved the effect she wanted. There are some good examples of this among the humorous stories.

One of these particularly enjoyed by her readers is "The Dulham Ladies" (*Atlantic*, April 1886), which has probably been more often reprinted in anthologies than anything else she ever wrote. This is a simple incident concerned with gentility, a quality important to the nineteenth century. Two aging sisters, the Miss Dobins (with one b), are unable to realize how much times have changed in their village. They suppose themselves still leaders in the community as they were in the days of their minister father. They become aware, one day, that with the years their hair has become very thin and they decide that it is their duty to society to supplement it with false fronts. Those imposed upon them by an amused salesman give them great pride and comfort. The idea that they might be ridiculous never occurs to them.

The two old ladies with their high intentions and innocent inability to comprehend reality are full of charm and their mistakes and miscalculations are really amusing but the story is somewhat less effective than it might be because the author is too obviously present pointing out the humor of their errors.

About two years after this, Miss Jewett, with admirable effect, tried letting the protagonist of a long story tell the major part of it. "Law Lane" (*Scribner's*, December 1887) has perhaps the neatest plot she ever succeeded in making. It is a story of neighboring families who have carried on a feud through several generations over a certain strip of property. (New England feuds are less likely to explode into physical violence than those of the West and South but they can be full of stubbornness and venom.) A Romeo and Juliet love springs up between a son and daughter of the present generation which is finally brought to a happy conclusion by the principal teller of the tale, Mrs. Harriet Powder. She is a famous nurse and is called in to help when the boy's mother has a dangerous fall in her cellar. The shock is so great that the patient is sure she is going to die, a notion which Mrs. Powder skillfully encourages until the suffering woman has remorsefully repented of the long quarrel and forgiven everybody — her neighbors and her son. Both sides are thankful to have the feud over and have no suspicions concerning Mrs. Powder, whose lively speech makes the story of her intrigue thoroughly entertaining.

Six years after "Law Lane" Miss Jewett tried another device which worked even better. She is telling a story which, like "The Dulham Ladies," is about two elderly women. She lets them make the humorous nature of their situation clear as they talk to one another. "The Guests of Mrs. Timms" (*Century*, February 1894) have met, at a church conference, an old acquaintance who is so friendly and hospitable in pressing them to spend a day with her soon that they decide to go the next week. But they discover, after the long bus ride, that they are neither expected nor wanted, as their hostess makes politely clear by her formal reception, taking it for granted that they have come to town on other business and are merely making her a morning call.

In the stories of autumn courtships which Miss Jewett liked to write there are some significant advances from sentimentality to humor and even irony. In one particularly successful story she carries the romantic sentiments of maturity further still. "The Only Rose" (*Atlantic*, January 1894) is one of the best stories Sarah Jewett wrote. It describes not the humor nor the volcanoes under the New England crust but some of the buried romance and sentiment which seldom get put into words.

Mrs. Bickford, presented by a gardening sister with a great mass of flowers, decides to make them into three "bo'quets" to place on the graves of her three husbands. She would go by the cemetery tomorrow when her favorite nephew comes to drive her over to spend the day with his family. An early flowering plant of her own has just produced a single rose and her great moral problem is to which of the three bouquets it should be added. To a neighbor so self-effacing that talking to her is like thinking aloud, she details the characteristics of the three men, trying, like a good New Englander, to do them each justice. To her last husband, Mr. B, she is grateful for leaving her so comfortably provided for but he "done everything by rule an' measure" and he "used 'most always to sleep in the evenin's." With Mr. Wallis, her second husband, living was often precarious because he was an unsuccessful inventor. He had all sorts of ingenious ideas which he never managed to bring to practical shape but he was a fluent talker and "splendid company for winter evenings." Albert she had married when they were both very young but "we was dreadful happy." Even overnight Mrs. Bickford cannot solve her problem.

It was settled for her next day by the nephew who carried the bouquets up the steep hillside and placed them on the graves. Suddenly Mrs. Bickford's heart felt lighter. "I know," she said to herself, "who I do hope's got the right one." The boy comes back with the red rose in his buttonhole. This fell out, he says, "an' I kept it. . . . I can give it to Lizzie." He has been telling his aunt of his engagement. "My first husband was just such a tall, straight young man as you be," she says to him. "The flower he first give me was a rose."

With the far more difficult problem of handling a subject somewhat beyond the confines of everyday life Sarah Jewett tried many interesting experiments. Not all of them are successful but it is fascinating to watch how her skill increased as she made one trial after another, as she matured and her literary ability improved.

One of the early attempts in this kind, "The Landscape Chamber" (*Atlantic*, November 1887), suggests more definitely than anything else she wrote a desire to do something in the manner of Hawthorne. It is the story of a curse.

The narrator is refreshing herself after a tiresome summer by a long horseback journey into country she has never visited before. One afternoon her horse is lamed by a small accident and she asks for lodging at a lonely handsome old house which seems to be disintegrating from poverty and neglect. The inhabitants are an aging father, whose manner suggests that he is a miser, and a pathetically agreeing daughter who accepts his penuriousness but covers it a little with immaculate housekeeping and a lovingly tended flower bed. Both seem solitary and without hope but rouse the narrator's interest and compassion. The father finally tells her of the curse which fell upon the family when an ancestor sold his soul for wealth. Since that day "we cannot part with what we have, even for common comfort."

Using the bright autumn landscape as contrast Miss Jewett succeeds in conveying the air of mystery and doom about the old house and its inhabitants. She weakens her effect somewhat by having the narrator admit that she thinks the father "not quite sane" but the daughter's last words restore the tone: "I think we shall all disappear some night in a winter storm, and the world will be rid of us, — father and the house and I, all three."

Far more complex and difficult was the problem Sarah Jewett posed for herself in "A White Heron" (1886). This is a story for which she herself cared greatly but which the *Atlantic* refused to print. The editor's reason, one supposes, was that though it has passages of excellent writing, the story as a whole — this happened rarely with Miss Jewett — is better than the telling of it.

"A White Heron" is one of the earliest conservation stories but it is conservation based not on practical twentieth-century arguments but on the sense of a mystical kinship between Man and Nature, a kinship which Miss Jewett felt very strongly herself.

The heroine of the story is a lonely little girl who lives with her grandmother on an isolated farm. Having no other playmates she has made friends with all sorts of birds and small animals.

A handsome young ornithologist, hunting in the woods, spends a few days with them and Sylvy takes a romantic delight in his company despite his shooting of her bird friends. He wants especially to find a great white heron. Sylvy thinks she knows where his nest is. She gets up very early one morning, takes a long walk, and makes a difficult and dangerous climb of a tall pine tree from which she can see the sun rising over the glistening sea. Then from the marsh far below a great white heron "like a single floating feather comes up from the dead hemlock and grows larger, and rises, and comes close at last, and goes by the landmark pine with steady sweep of wing and outstretched slender neck and crested head." Sylvy feels that she has shared with him the experience of that wonderful sunrise.

Soberly she makes her way home, her young mind struggling with ideas and emotions she has never experienced before. The handsome young man says that he must leave that afternoon but Sylvy cannot tell him what she has discovered, she cannot violate her mystic moment of communion with the great white bird and bring him to his death. Miss Jewett when she tries to express these emotions finds herself bereft of her usual quiet skill. She uses the false self-conscious rhetoric all too common among her contemporaries. She even resorts to that disastrous device of addressing her character directly: "And wait! wait! do not move a foot or a finger, little girl, do not send an arrow of light and consciousness from your two eager eyes, for the heron has perched on a pine bough not far beyond yours."

Fifteen years later Sarah Jewett was handling a not dissimilar theme with simplicity and skill. This time it is a matter of communication with the dead, a possibility in which she firmly believed. Her faith in personal immortality was sure. She was certain, too, that the souls of the departed watch over those they have loved on earth. The story of "The Foreigner" (*Atlantic,* August 1900) is told by Mrs. Almira Todd, the herbwoman of Dunnet Landing who is the chief character in *The Country of the Pointed Firs.*

When Cap'n Tolland brought home from the West Indies a young French wife who found it difficult to adapt to New England ways, Almira Todd, then a young woman, was one of the few in the village who tried to be a friend to her. When the Captain was lost at sea the poor little wife sank into a decline and Mrs. Todd helped to nurse and sustain her through her last days. Not long before her death her dead mother appears to her. "All of a sudden," says Mrs. Todd, "she set right up in bed with her eyes wide open . . . And she reached out both her arms toward the door, an' I looked the way she was lookin', an' I see some one was standin' there against the dark. . . . 't was a woman's dark face lookin' right at us; 't wa'n't but an instant I could see. I felt dreadful cold, and my head begun to swim; I thought the light went out; 't wa'n't but an instant, as I say, an' when my sight come back I could n't see nothing there."

The solution here is much like that by which Sarah Jewett had improved the telling of her humorous sketches, entrusting the description of strange events and strong emotions to one of the actors in the story. The same solution helped in the suppression of sentimentality, over which she finally achieved full control. In *The Country of the Pointed Firs* which is always, and correctly, spoken of as her finest work, she is able to make her pronouncements in either the assistant narrator's voice or in the narrator's, that is her own, without overstepping any bounds.

The Country of the Pointed Firs (1896) is not a novel and not much seems to be gained by calling it, as some modern critics are inclined to do, a para-novel, but it does have a definite and effective unity. This is achieved by methods reminiscent of *Deephaven* but employed with far more sophistication so that the community of Dunnet Landing is not only a definite seacoast village but an epitome of the whole state of Maine. Between the covers of this remarkable little book one can find, indeed, almost the whole of New England, its landscape, its social changes, its people and their special qualities. Sarah Jewett did not deliberately set out to do anything of the kind but it was at this moment that her long observation and study of her country, her long practice in writing of everyday life as though it were history, came to its climax. It is with *The Country of the Pointed Firs* that one should begin to read the work of Sarah Orne Jewett.

Henry James, who admired the book, once asked Miss Jewett whether Dunnet Landing was a real place and when she replied that she had invented it, he nodded in approval, murmuring, "I thought so." To less discerning inquirers she said that "it must be somewhere 'along shore' between the region of Tenants Harbor and Boothbay." The sketches which make up the book were published in four installments in the *Atlantic Monthly*. Each of these groups can stand alone but they seem to have been composed on a definite connecting pattern. Four later sketches set in Dunnet Landing, which were added to the book in posthumous editions, are perfectly consistent in tone but fall outside the time sequence of the pattern, which runs from June to September. One is always conscious of the background, the firs, the balsams, the rocks, the birds and bushes, the constantly changing aspects of the sea, but it is never overemphasized.

The narrator is played down so that she provides only the necessary curiosity, questions, and responses. The important figure is the assistant narrator, one of the best characters, as I have said, Miss Jewett ever drew. She is the narrator's landlady, Mrs.

Almira Todd, herbwoman of the village, and much of the book is told in her distinctive and effective speech. As she and the narrator come to know each other well they develop a real friendship so that Mrs. Todd reveals something of her inner life. There is no volcano beneath her granite but a deep accepted grief. She had loved above her station. "He come of a high family, an' my lot was plain an' hard-workin'." "His mother didn't favor the match, an' done everything she could to part us; and folks thought we both married well, but 't wa'n't what either one of us wanted most."

The man Almira married, though she could never give him her heart, was lost at sea not long after their wedding. She took to herb-doctoring, at which she was skilled, and made herself a good living and an important position in the community. She knows its history and the details of the lives of most of her neighbors and is agreeably outspoken about their faults and virtues.

As the narrator has been made less conspicuous than she is in *Deephaven* and the language of the book has been made simpler and more precise, so the number of subsidiary characters has been reduced to a few of real significance. In all these characters Miss Jewett is presenting the New England qualities she has been describing in her other stories: endurance, courage, independence, industry, conscientiousness, and her own belief in the happy interest to be found in the commonplaces of day-to-day living.

The clearest exponent of Dunnet Landing's decline since it ceased to be a seaport is Captain Littlepage, long retired but full of pregnant ideas as well as strange fanciful thoughts. According to Mrs. Todd his mind has been unhinged by too much reading. He is devoted to Milton and Shakespeare. A curious experience in an Arctic shipwreck has left him with the conviction that he knows the location of a strange city, the waiting place for spirits between earth and heaven, but about the changes in the Landing he is quite lucid. "In the old days a good part o' the best men here knew a hundred ports and something of the way folks lived in them. They saw the world for themselves, and like's not their wives and children saw it with them. . . . they got some sense o' proportion."

Mr. Tilley, once a fisherman, keeps his balance by cherishing the memory of his lovable and capable wife who died eight years ago. He keeps everything in his neat little house as nearly as possible in the way "poor dear" liked to have it. There is also the curious tale of Poor Joanna of Shell-heap Island, one of the solitaries already mentioned. She became a hermit but maintained her dignity and her personality. Significant also is the way in which the community respects her way of life without prying or making unjustified attempts to dissuade her.

Most important of all is Mrs. Todd's octogenarian mother, Mrs. Blackett, who lives with her shy fisherman son on one of the outer islands. Its name, Green Island, suggests that it is a kind of little paradise. Mrs. Blackett enjoys nature and her daily life so thoroughly that she refreshes every friend with whom she comes in contact.

The Country of the Pointed Firs brought Miss Jewett enthusiastic approval both from the critics and from her friends. The most precise assessment of all came in a letter from William James. The book, he said, has "that incommunicable cleanness of the salt air when one first leaves town," and this is a quality one is refreshed by in most of Miss Jewett's work.

Agreeable as she found it to have this kind of written and spoken praise and to find herself treated as a distinguished literary lady of Boston, what Sarah Jewett enjoyed most all through her professional life were the tributes from her own state of Maine. She was much pleased when from time to time on May 30 South Berwick included in its official exercises a reading of her

"Decoration Day." This is a simple tale of how, some twenty-five years after the war, the nine Union soldiers who are still alive in the little village of Barlow Plains decide that the community, small as it is, ought to honor its soldier dead, of their brave procession through the countryside, planting a flag on each grave, and of how the people of Barlow rise to the occasion.

But the distinction Miss Jewett cared for most of all was the honorary Litt.D., the first the college ever conferred upon a woman, which Bowdoin granted her in 1901. "You can't think," she wrote Mrs. Fields, "how nice it was to be the single sister of so many brothers."

In 1902 Miss Jewett had a serious accident, a fall from a carriage which severely injured her neck and spine and left her with greatly depleted energy. She kept up her friendships and her correspondence vigorously. A particularly happy note here was the acquaintance, which grew into a real friendship, with the young Willa Cather who had, she thought, great promise. But though letters were possible Sarah Jewett was never able to write another story.

In March 1909 she had a stroke while staying with Mrs. Fields and asked to be taken home to Berwick. Her death occurred on June 24, 1909. Some years before she had said in speaking of the old house: "I was born here and I hope to die here, leaving the lilac bushes still green and growing and all the chairs in their places." She could not have made herself a better epitaph; this was not only an exposition of the way she liked to order her life but of the literary creed by which she tried to order her writing.

⤳ Selected Bibliography

Works of Sarah Orne Jewett

COLLECTIONS OF SHORT STORIES

Deephaven. Boston: James R. Osgood, 1877. (Reissued by Houghton, Mifflin in 1894, with a new Preface by the author.)

Old Friends and New. Boston: Houghton, Osgood, 1879.

Country By-Ways. Boston: Houghton, Mifflin, 1881.

The Mate of the Daylight, and Friends Ashore. Boston and New York: Houghton, Mifflin, 1884.

A White Heron and Other Stories. Boston and New York: Houghton, Mifflin, 1886.

The King of Folly Island and Other People. Boston and New York: Houghton, Mifflin, 1888.

Strangers and Wayfarers. Boston and New York: Houghton, Mifflin, 1890.

Tales of New England. Boston and New York: Houghton, Mifflin, 1890. (Collected from the preceding volumes.)

A Native of Winby and Other Tales. Boston and New York: Houghton, Mifflin, 1893.

The Life of Nancy. Boston and New York: Houghton, Mifflin, 1895.

The Country of the Pointed Firs. Boston and New York: Houghton, Mifflin, 1896.

The Queen's Twin and Other Stories. Boston and New York: Houghton, Mifflin, 1899.

Stories and Tales. 7 volumes. Boston: Houghton, Mifflin, 1910.

The Best Stories of Sarah Orne Jewett, edited, with a Preface, by Willa Cather. 2 volumes. Boston: Houghton, Mifflin, 1925. Volume 1 contains *The Country of the Pointed Firs*.

The Only Rose and Other Tales, edited, with an Introduction, by Rebecca West. London: Jonathan Cape, 1937.

NOVELS

A Country Doctor. Boston and New York: Houghton, Mifflin, 1884.

A Marsh Island. Boston and New York: Houghton, Mifflin, 1885.

The Tory Lover. Boston and New York: Houghton, Mifflin, 1901.

Selected Bibliography

STORIES FOR CHILDREN

Play Days: A Book of Stories for Children. Boston: Houghton, Osgood, 1878.
The Story of the Normans, Told Chiefly in Relation to Their Conquest of England. New York and London: G. P. Putnam's Sons, 1887.
Betty Leicester: A Story for Girls. Boston and New York: Houghton, Mifflin, 1890.
Betty Leicester's Christmas. Boston and New York: Houghton, Mifflin, 1899.

VERSE

Verses, Printed for Her Friends. Boston: Merrymount Press, 1916.

LETTERS

Letters of Sarah Orne Jewett, edited by Annie Fields. Boston and New York: Houghton, Mifflin, 1911.
Sarah Orne Jewett Letters, edited by Richard Cary. Waterville, Maine: Colby College Press, 1956.

CURRENT AMERICAN REPRINTS

The Country of the Pointed Firs and Other Stories, edited, with a Preface, by Willa Cather. Garden City, N.Y.: Anchor (Doubleday). $.95.
The World of Dunnet Landing, edited by David Bonnell Green. Lincoln: University of Nebraska Press. $1.75. (Contains *The Country of the Pointed Firs*, four additional Dunnet Landing stories, and five critical essays by Warner Berthoff, Mary Ellen Chase, David Bonnell Green, Martha Hale Shackford, and Hyatt H. Waggoner.)

Bibliographies

Frost, John Eldridge. "Sarah Orne Jewett Bibliography: 1949–1963," *Colby Library Quarterly*, Series 6, No. 10 (June 1964), pp. 405–17.
Spiller, Robert E., *et al.*, eds. *Literary History of the United States: Bibliography*. Third edition revised. New York: Macmillan, 1963. Pp. 602–4. *Supplement*. 1964. Pp. 152–53.
Weber, Clara Carter, and Charles J. Weber. *A Bibliography of the Published Writings of Sarah Orne Jewett*. Waterville, Maine: Colby College Press, 1949.

Biographical and Critical Studies

Auchincloss, Louis. "Sarah Orne Jewett," in *Pioneers and Caretakers*. Minneapolis: University of Minnesota Press, 1965.

47

Berthoff, Warner. "The Art of Jewett's *Pointed Firs*," *New England Quarterly*, 32:31–53 (March 1959).

Bishop, Ferman. "Henry James Criticizes *The Tory Lover*," *American Literature*, 27:262–64 (May 1955).

————. "Sarah Orne Jewett's Idea of Race," *New England Quarterly*, 30: 243–49 (June 1957).

Buchan, A. M. *"Our Dear Sarah": An Essay on Sarah Orne Jewett*. Washington University Studies, No. 24. St. Louis, Missouri, 1953.

Cary, Richard. *Sarah Orne Jewett* (United States Authors Series). New York: Twayne, 1962.

Cather, Willa. "Miss Jewett," in *Not under Forty*. New York: Knopf, 1936.

Chapman, Edward M. "The New England of Sarah Orne Jewett," *Yale Review*, n.s., 3:157–72 (October 1913).

Chase, Mary Ellen. "Sarah Orne Jewett as a Social Historian," in *The World of Dunnet Landing*, edited by David Bonnell Green. Lincoln: University of Nebraska Press, 1962.

Frost, John Eldridge. *Sarah Orne Jewett*. Kittery Point, Maine: Gundalow Club, 1960.

Green, David Bonnell. "The World of Dunnet Landing," *New England Quarterly*, 34:514–17 (December 1961).

Howe, M. A. De Wolfe. "Sarah Orne Jewett," in *Memories of a Hostess*. Boston: Atlantic Monthly Press, 1922. (Drawn chiefly from the diaries of Mrs. James T. Fields.)

Jewett, Sarah Orne. "Looking Back on Girlhood," *Youth's Companion*, 65: 5–6 (January 7, 1892).

Magowan, Robin. "Pastoral and the Art of Landscape in *The Country of the Pointed Firs*," *New England Quarterly*, 32:229–40 (June 1963).

Matthiessen, F. O. *Sarah Orne Jewett*. Boston and New York: Houghton, Mifflin, 1929. (Matthiessen also contributed the biographical sketch to the *Dictionary of American Biography*, 1933.)

Shackford, Martha Hale. "Sarah Orne Jewett," *Sewanee Review*, 30:20–26 (January 1922).

Short, Clarice. "Studies in Gentleness," *Western Humanities Review*, 11: 387–93 (Autumn 1957).

Smith, Eleanor M. "The Literary Relationship of Sarah Orne Jewett and Willa Sibert Cather," *New England Quarterly*, 29:472–92 (December 1956).

Thompson, Charles M. "The Art of Miss Jewett," *Atlantic Monthly*, 94:485–97 (October 1904).

Waggoner, Hyatt H. "The Unity of *The Country of the Pointed Firs*," *Twentieth Century Literature*, 5:67–73 (July 1959).

Weber, Carl J. "Whittier and Sarah Orne Jewett," *New England Quarterly*, 18:401–7 (September 1945).

UNIVERSITY OF MINNESOTA
PAMPHLETS ON AMERICAN WRITERS

William Van O'Connor, Allen Tate, Leonard Unger, and Robert Penn
Warren, editors. Willard Thorp, Karl Shapiro, and Philip Rahv, advisers

EACH PAMPHLET, 65 CENTS

UNIVERSITY OF MINNESOTA PRESS, Minneapolis, Minnesota 55455, U.S.A.